SOLO PLUS

Violin

W0007397

Cover photography by Randall Wallace
Arranged and performed by David Pearl

Order No. AM 967604
US International Standard Book Number: 0.8256.1820.7
UK International Standard Book Number: 0.7119.8516.2

Exclusive Distributors:
Music Sales Corporation
257 Park Avenue South, New York, NY 10010 USA
Music Sales Limited
8/9 Frith Street, London W1D 3JB England
Music Sales Pty. Limited
120 Rothschild Street, Rosebery, Sydney, NSW 2018, Australia

Printed in the United States of America by
Vicks Lithograph and Printing Corporation

Amsco Publications
New York/London/Paris/Sydney/Copenhagen/Madrid

Angels We Have Heard on High

Traditional French carol

Deck the Hall

Traditional Welsh carol

The First Noel

Traditional English carol

It Came Upon a Midnight Clear

Richard Storrs Willis (1819–1900)

Go, Tell It on the Mountain

Traditional African-American spiritual

God Rest Ye Merry, Gentlemen

Traditional English carol

I Wonder as I Wander

John Jacob Niles (1892–1980)

Jingle Bells

James S. Pierpont (1822–1893)

O Come, All Ye Faithful

Adeste Fidelis

Traditional English carol

O, Holy Night

Adolphe Adam (1803–1856)

O Little Town of Bethlehem

Lewis H. Redner (1831–1908)

The Babe of Bethle'm

Traditional English carol

Silent Night

Franz X. Gruber (1787–1863)

What Child Is This?

Greensleeves

Traditional English air

Rocking

Traditional Czech carol